Athletics

Written by Andy Seed

Contents

Collins

What is athletics?

Athletics is a sport with lots of events.

You can see:

competitors jumping
objects in flight
winners claiming medals
CANADA

Sprinting

Sprinters run
in a quick
burst of speed.

At the start, they power off from the starting block.

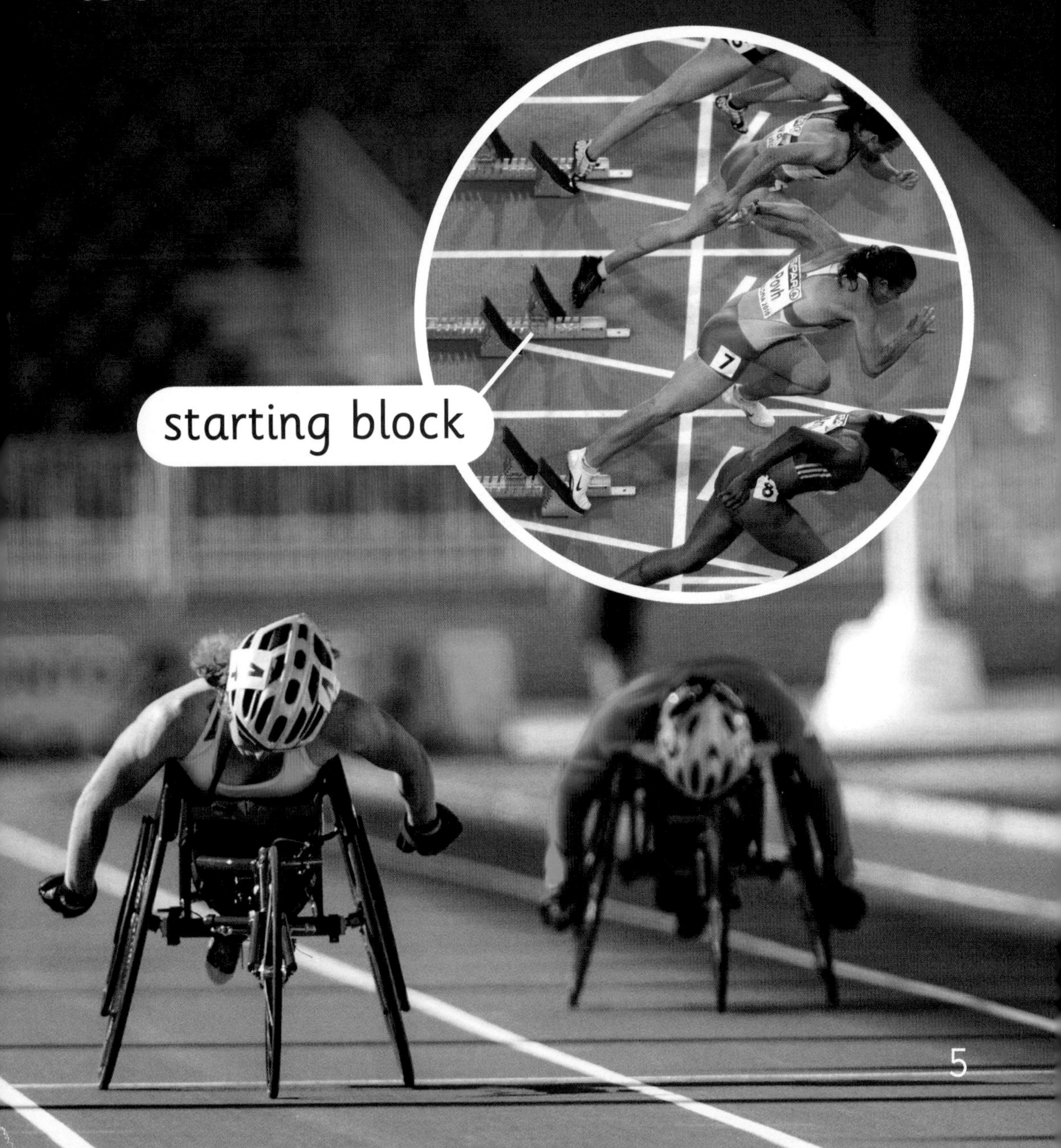

Marathon

In a marathon, competitors train hard to run much further.

They must not rush at the start but can sprint as they speed to the finish.

The crowd claps to support the winner.

High jump

Competitors approach the high jump with a short run.

They jump up and twist in the air to clear the crossbar.

The highest jumper claims a medal.

Long jump

The long jump starts with a rapid sprint. This boosts the jumpers as they spring up.

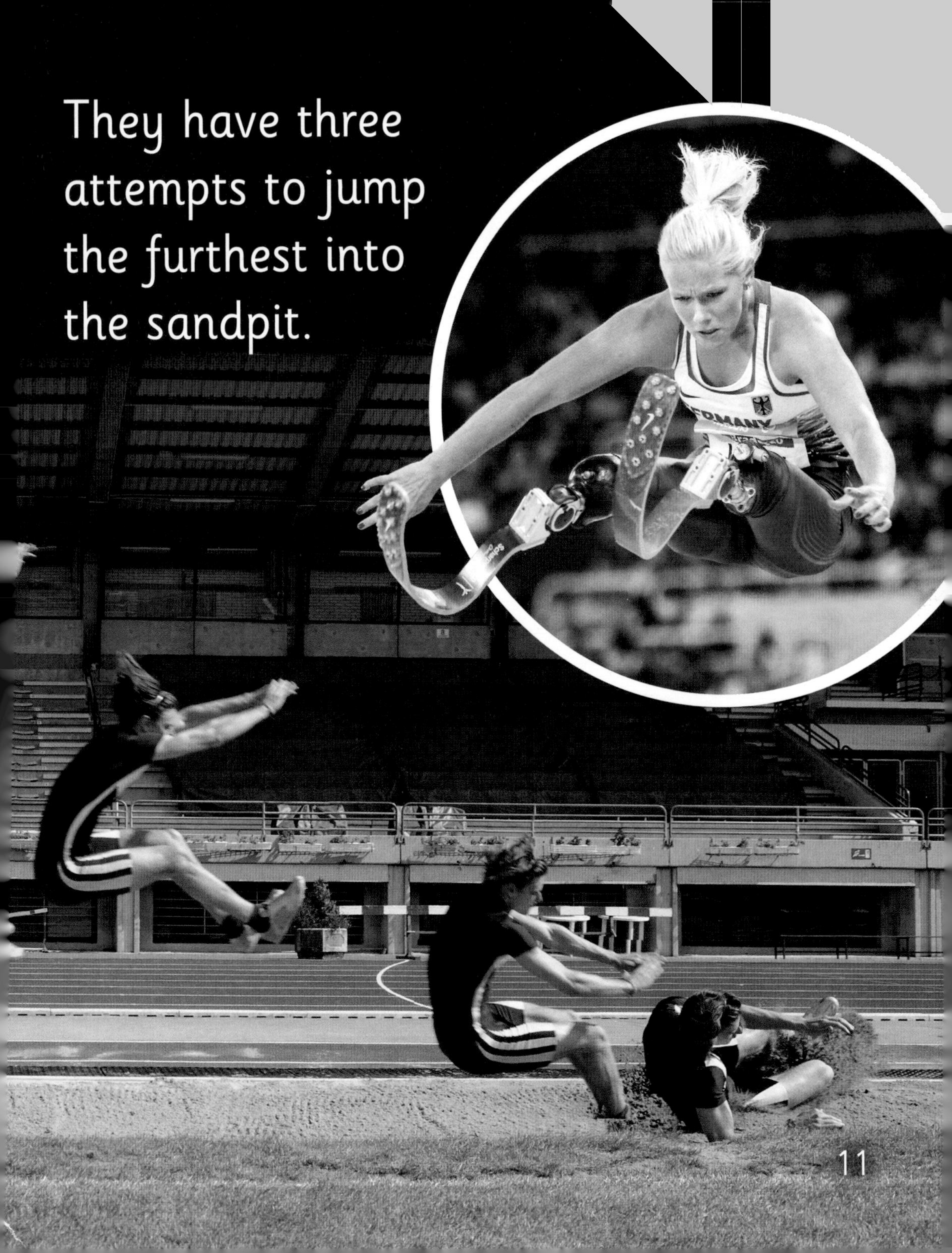

They have three attempts to jump the furthest into the sandpit.

Discus

Competitors spin with the discus, and then hurl it into the air.

The competitor that lands the discus the furthest is the victor.

The discus is a blur
as it speeds from
the competitor's hand.

Athletics events

Jumping
High jump
Long jump
Hurling
Discus
Allianz
KARAM JYOTI
LONDON 2017

◂36

After reading

Letters and Sounds: Phase 4

Word count: 183

Focus on adjacent consonants with long vowel phonemes e.g. /s/ /p/ /ee/ /d/

Common exception words: of, to, the, into, you, they, have, what

Curriculum links: Mathematics: Measurement

National Curriculum learning objectives: Spoken language: articulate and justify answers, arguments and opinions; Reading/Word reading: apply phonic knowledge and skills as the route to decode words, read accurately by blending sounds in unfamiliar words containing GPCs that have been taught, read other words of more than one syllable that contain taught GPCs, read aloud accurately books that are consistent with their developing phonic knowledge; Reading/Comprehension: understand both the books they can already read accurately and fluently ... by: drawing on what they already know or on background information and vocabulary provided by the teacher

Developing fluency

- Your child may enjoy hearing you read the book. Model reading with lots of expression.
- You may wish to take turns to read a page.

Phonic practice

- Look at page 2 together. Ask your child:
  - Can you find two words that start with the two consonants **s** and **p**? (e.g. *sport*, *sprinting*)
  - Can you think of any other words that start with the two consonants **s** and **p**? (e.g. *spoon*, *speed*, *spear*)
- Now look at page 6. Ask your child:
  - Can you find a word that starts with the two consonants **t** and **r**? (*train*)
  - Can you think of any other words that start with the two consonants **t** and **r**? (e.g. *tree*, *trick*, *trail*)

Extending vocabulary

- Read page 10 to your child. Ask them if they can think of another word that could be used instead of **spring**? (e.g. *jump*, *leap*)
- Read page 12 to your child. Ask them if they can think of another word that could be used instead of 'victor'? (e.g. *winner*)